Praise for *Things We Desire*

"Around the turn of the seventh decade of the last century, a time of violence and of disorienting change, a calming list of advisories called "Desiderata" went viral by the standards of the day. Posted, reprinted, and occasionally parodied, it was everywhere, and readers were divided on whether it was profound or kitsch. More than half a century later, in a new era of anxiety and confusion, Tony tells the story behind this cultural icon and invites us to savor its wisdom and serenity."

— *Steven Pinker*
Johnstone Family Professor of Psychology
Harvard University

"In a world of pressure and noise, this book is a much-needed timeout. The timeless truths of "Desiderata", brought to life in these pages by Tony in a way that offers calm perspective and grounded guidance. It's a playbook for the soul—one I'll be keeping close."

— *Nick Nurse*
Head Coach, Philadelphia 76ers

"Tony has done it again. His insight into things that really matter is stunning! "Things We Desire" is a must read!!"

— *Dr. Jim Loehr*
World-renowned performance psychologist,
New York Times *bestselling author, Co-founder, Coach*
Leading with Character, always

"Tony has distilled timeless truths into a powerful guide for living with purpose and grace. "Things We Desire" transforms the Desiderata's wisdom into actionable steps for today's seekers."

— *Dr. Alan Zimmerman*
Inducted into the "Speaker Hall of Fame" and "Legends of Speaking"

Also by Tony D. Thelen

"Am I Doing This Right? Foundations for
a Successful Career and a Fulfilling Life"
(Business Expert Press, NY, 2022)

"The River—30 Articles
to Advance Your Career and Life"
(The River Press, 2024)

THINGS WE DESIRE

THE DESIDERATA TURNS ONE HUNDRED

TONY D. THELEN

Things We Desire

Copyright © 2025 by The River Press
All rights reserved.

No part of this book may be reproduced or used in any manner without written permission of the copyright owner except for the use of quotations in a book review.

E-mail: tony@therivercoach.org

For more information, go to
www.therivercoach.org

Cover design by Shivam Mehta
Book design by Alan Barnett
Edited by Elizabeth Maynard Charle & Katherine Evans

ISBN 979-8-9998456-0-3 (paperback)
ISBN 979-8-9998456-1-0 (hardcover)
ISBN 979-8-9998456-2-7 (ebook)

*For Shirley—sister, artist, writer, dreamer—
your way of seeing the world has always reminded me
how much there is to cherish, create, and become.*

*Your life has inspired me beyond
words, pictures, and paintings.*

CONTENTS

What People Say ix

"Desiderata" x

Foreword xiii

Introduction 1

Calm 5

Peace 9

Harmony 13

Truth 17

Listen 21

Serenity 25

Contentment 29

Acceptance 33

Joy 37

Purpose 41

Stability 45

Prudence 49

Contents

Awareness 53

Virtue 57

Aspiration 61

Courage 65

Authenticity 69

Sincerity 73

Love 77

Hope 81

Wisdom 85

Resilience 89

Positivity 93

Compassion 97

Belonging. 101

Trust. 105

Reverence 109

Focus 113

Beauty 117

Happiness 121

The River Career & Life Assessment™ 125

The Man Behind the Poem 127

About the Author. 131

What People Say

"If ever there was a secular scripture, 'Desiderata' is it."

— *Morgan Freeman*

"The message of 'Desiderata' aligns with what science shows us: we are children of the universe—connected, significant, and capable of peace."

— *Carl Sagan*

"There is a line from 'Desiderata' that has stayed with me for decades: 'You are a child of the universe…' That truth helps me feel grounded no matter what."

— *Oprah Winfrey*

"This poem reflects a human heart seeking peace, compassion, and truth. It is very beautiful."

— *Dalai Lama*

"I should like, if I could, to leave a humble gift—a bit of chaste prose that might suggest the universality of beauty and truth."

— *Max Ehrmann*

"DESIDERATA"

Go placidly amid the noise and haste,
and remember what peace there may be in silence.
As far as possible, without surrender, be
on good terms with all persons.

Speak your truth quietly and clearly; and listen to others, even
to the dull and the ignorant; they too have their story.

Avoid loud and aggressive persons; they are vexatious to the spirit.
If you compare yourself with others, you may become vain and bitter,
for always there will be greater and lesser persons than yourself.

Enjoy your achievements as well as your plans.
Keep interested in your own career, however humble;
it is a real possession in the changing fortunes of time.

Exercise caution in your business affairs,
for the world is full of trickery.
But let this not blind you to what virtue there is;
many persons strive for high ideals,
and everywhere life is full of heroism.

Be yourself. Especially, do not feign affection.
Neither be cynical about love; for in the face of all aridity
and disenchantment, it is as perennial as the grass.

Take kindly the counsel of the years,
gracefully surrendering the things of youth.
Nurture strength of spirit to shield you in sudden misfortune.
But do not distress yourself with dark imaginings.
Many fears are born of fatigue and loneliness.

Desiderata

Beyond a wholesome discipline, be gentle with yourself.
You are a child of the universe no less than the trees and the stars;
you have a right to be here.

And whether or not it is clear to you,
no doubt the universe is unfolding as it should.

Therefore be at peace with God, whatever you
conceive Him to be, and whatever your labors and aspirations,
in the noisy confusion of life, keep peace in your soul.

With all its sham, drudgery and
broken dreams, it is still a beautiful world.
Be cheerful. Strive to be happy.

— Max Ehrmann, 1927

FOREWORD

Sometimes, the best meetings aren't planned—they just happen, and later you realize they were exactly what was needed. That's how it was when I met Tony Thelen at Deere & Company. We met at a work event where I was visiting as a board member. The timing was random, unpredictable, and yet perfect. Tony was retiring within a few weeks of our meeting, and my journey as a board member was just beginning. Without that chance moment, our paths would have never crossed. At this time, I was early in my post-corporate career, still trying to understand where I could make the most meaningful impact in my next season. Tony credited the poem "Desiderata" with guiding his own personal and professional journey over his three decades of dedicated service.

Truthfully, I had never read "Desiderata" until our conversation, but the way he spoke about its influence on his life and family were contagious. I knew I had to read it for myself.

As I reflected on the poem, I was reminded of a prayer a friend shared with me. During his darkest hour, as he faced the loss of his beloved wife to pancreatic cancer, he expressed his gratitude for me. He asked that I never lose the ability to smile. The prayer he shared focused on joy and positivity—two central themes of "Desiderata."

"Heavenly Father—Thank you for the opportunity to laugh. Help me find joy in all I do. Let me laugh and be cheerful so that those around me will be blessed by my optimism and smile."

This prayer resonates with me because it reinforces a central belief: how we approach life will have a direct, positive impact on others. You see, I have a deep desire to bring joy to those around me, not as a cheerleader or people-pleaser, but truly to be a genuine light in other people's life. That spirit—of optimism and embracing life—is a cornerstone for how I live. When doubts and fears inevitably arise, I remind myself that how I show up can make a difference.

Reading *Things We Desire*, reminded me how I was raised to live a good life. Tony's celebration of the centennial of this poem offers more than inspiration—it is a practical blueprint for how we can not only live a good life, but truly *enjoy* the journey as well. In my corporate life we often said we wanted people to have both a great career AND a great life. Tony puts it this way, "A's at home and A's at work." Tony has taken the soul of this poem and created a guide that can be used for daily, weekly, or monthly reflection. He has broken the poem into key behaviors, reinforcing that each of us has the ability to decide how we want to live—not by chance, but by choice.

After I read *Things We Desire*, I realized my own life's motto of living with "grit, gumption, grace, and gratitude" stared back at me. It struck me I had been leading a "Desiderata life" in my own way for years. Each of us chooses how we live, love, and lead. It's our ultimate superpower to lead our lives on our terms, in our own special way. As my personal and professional life took shape, I found the combination of grit, gumption, grace, and gratitude to be my true north.

My parents taught me to work hard and believe in myself. But alone, these were not enough. My mother taught me early in life that how you win is as important as how you lose, and that while people understand a bad loser, no one ever forgets a bad winner. Grace and gratitude are not enough on their own; you need grit and gumption. These four words have not just shaped my journey; they have become the unwavering compass for how I strive to live in both my professional as well as personal life.

I was fortunate to work in the same industry—and at the same company—where my parents met. I was blessed to be on the front line watching the ups and downs of my father's own professional journey. As my career grew, I discovered the grit and gumption inside of me. It was there all along. I learned I had inside of me what it takes to succeed, and I am proud of how I rose to meet the many challenges and pressures of executive leadership. I look back on my career with pride, knowing that while it wasn't always easy, I didn't just survive, I thrived.

Personally, nothing changes your perspective like hearing the words, "you have cancer." The worst thoughts come to mind, and everything you thought was important fades away. In that moment, grace and gratitude have a new meaning, strengthened by grit and gumption. As scared as I was, I was always reminded that many faced treatments that were more challenging, with less hopeful prognosis. I became aware that many of us never acknowledge the illness; rather, we present a positive view for the world to see as we don't want to be defined by the disease. Most importantly I was reminded how important it is to give grace to others since we never know what private battles others face.

For me, grit, gumption, grace and gratitude are more than words; they are my compass, shaped by family and friends and life's quiet lessons. They have given me resilience and optimism, just as "Desiderata" has done for so many over the past century.

Tony's *Things We Desire* is a gift for lifelong learners, for those with inspirable spirits. It's for anyone yearning for deeper serenity and inner peace while also passionately pursuing growth and progress in their lives. It is designed to be a deeply personal companion, a heartfelt gift of encouragement, or simply that perfect coffee table book you can pick up for a few minutes of profound wisdom and inspiration.

My wish is that after reading *Things We Desire,* you feel uplifted, empowered, and better equipped to embrace the beauty and purpose of your own life. I hope this book encourages you to lead, love, and live fully and on your terms (and perhaps with a bit of grit, gumption, grace, and gratitude).

— Leanne G. Caret
Oct 2025

INTRODUCTION

In 1969, my oldest sister, Shirley, was a senior in high school. She had recently learned calligraphy in her art class, and the instructor gave her an assignment to create something with her newly developed skills. She chose to make an elegant copy of the poem, "Desiderata", by Max Ehrmann. In the early 1980s this poem hung in my bedroom throughout my high school years.

And so began my relationship with the "Desiderata" for the rest of my life.

I remember reading it, mesmerized by its emotion and sense of serenity. It seemed written for me during the most critical times of my life. Beyond the moments of self-doubt or personal crisis, the poem called me to aspire to a life well-lived, not only toward professional success, but personal fulfillment.

In the years following my introduction to the poem, I graduated high school and college, got a job, married, had three wonderful daughters, retired, and started my own executive coaching firm. The poem, and all its advice on life, has been my quiet advisor the entire journey.

In 2014, my mother passed away at the age of eighty-one, two years after my father had passed away at the age of seventy-nine. My three brothers and two sisters gathered to discuss what to do with the lifetime of artifacts my parents kept at the home they had moved into forty-seven years earlier. We went through everything and kept the most cherished of items, and the rest was either donated or disposed of.

Somewhere nearing the end of this process, my oldest brother, Ed, took one last look at the pile of things destined for disposal. He saw in that pile a lifetime of bits and pieces, every one of them holding a memory and having a reason for being there. Beneath the miscellaneous items, Ed spotted something. Carefully, he fished it out of the pile. And with this act, Shirley's original copy of the "Desiderata" had been saved. Ed carefully preserved the poem, and it has hung in his home ever since.

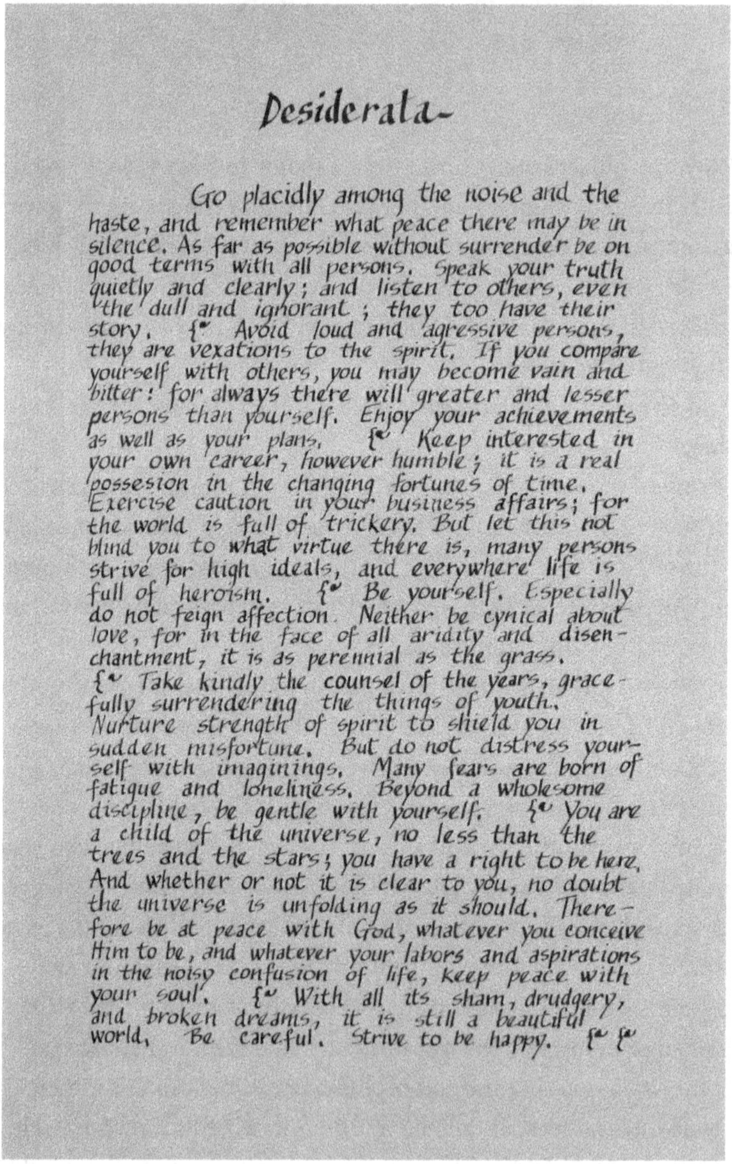

Desiderata-

Go placidly among the noise and the haste, and remember what peace there may be in silence. As far as possible without surrender be on good terms with all persons. Speak your truth quietly and clearly; and listen to others, even the dull and ignorant; they too have their story. Avoid loud and agressive persons, they are vexations to the spirit. If you compare yourself with others, you may become vain and bitter: for always there will greater and lesser persons than yourself. Enjoy your achievements as well as your plans. Keep interested in your own career, however humble; it is a real possesion in the changing fortunes of time. Exercise caution in your business affairs; for the world is full of trickery. But let this not blind you to what virtue there is, many persons strive for high ideals, and everywhere life is full of heroism. Be yourself. Especially do not feign affection. Neither be cynical about love, for in the face of all aridity and disenchantment, it is as perennial as the grass. Take kindly the counsel of the years, gracefully surrendering the things of youth. Nurture strength of spirit to shield you in sudden misfortune. But do not distress yourself with imaginings. Many fears are born of fatigue and loneliness. Beyond a wholesome discipline, be gentle with yourself. You are a child of the universe, no less than the trees and the stars; you have a right to be here, And whether or not it is clear to you, no doubt the universe is unfolding as it should. Therefore be at peace with God, whatever you conceive Him to be, and whatever your labors and aspirations in the noisy confusion of life, keep peace with your soul. With all its sham, drudgery, and broken dreams, it is still a beautiful world, Be careful. Strive to be happy.

Figure 1–The original art project from 1969 by the author's sister Shirley Neary

Introduction

"Desiderata", penned by Max Ehrmann in 1927, offers a roadmap for living with grace, purpose, and peace amid life's complexities. Its words resonate across generations, speaking to the universal human longing for meaning and serenity. This document distills the poem into twenty-four distinct elements; each paired with a focus word to illuminate its essence.

These elements serve as touchstones for reflection, guiding us through challenges like conflict, self-doubt, and the pursuit of happiness. By exploring each of these elements we connect the timeless wisdom embedded in Ehrmann's words to our own modern lives. Whether navigating a noisy world, seeking authenticity, or fostering resilience, "Desiderata" reminds us of the values that anchor a fulfilling life.

Ehrmann's counsel spans the personal and the universal, encouraging us to find calm amidst chaos, to speak our truth with clarity, and to embrace love despite life's hardships. Each section invites you to pause and reflect, offering practical insights for applying these lessons today. Together, these thirty elements form a holistic framework for cultivating inner peace, meaningful relationships, and a deep sense of purpose.

As you journey through this book, let each element inspire you to live with intention, aligning your actions with the timeless principles that lead to success and fulfillment in the one and only journey that counts in this world—your life.

Calm

"Go placidly amid the noise and haste ..."

In the opening line of "Desiderata", Max Ehrmann beckons us to "go placidly amid the noise and haste," a call to embody calm in a world often defined by chaos. This wisdom speaks to the modern struggle of constant stimulation—endless notifications, crowded schedules, and societal pressures that threaten our inner peace. To go placidly is to move with intention, refusing to be swept away by external turbulence.

It's not giving in, but more so standing and defending your right to live a life of peace and serenity.

Calmness becomes an act of quiet rebellion against the frenzy, a choice to prioritize serenity over reactivity. Imagine walking through a bustling city yet feeling an unshakable stillness within—like a lake undisturbed beneath a stormy sky.

This element teaches us that calm is not the absence of noise, but the presence of composure amidst it. To be calm is more than just an adjective; it's a defining character trait.

Practically, we might cultivate this by pausing to breathe deeply during a hectic day, grounding ourselves in the moment. Calmness fosters clarity, enabling us to respond thoughtfully rather than impulsively.

It's a reminder that we hold the power to shape our inner state, no matter the circumstances. We determine how we react to the world, not the events around us. By embracing calm, we create a sanctuary within, a space where we can navigate life's challenges from a position of power, and with grace.

How might you invite calm into your day?

BRINGING IT TO LIFE

Calm

- **Start Your Day with Intentional Stillness.**
  Begin each morning with five to ten minutes of quiet breathing or meditation before checking your phone or engaging with the world. This sets a calm foundation for the rest of your day.

- **Practice the 4-7-8 Breathing Technique.**
  Use this proven calming breath cycle (inhale four seconds, hold seven, exhale eight) whenever you feel stress or tension rising. Doing this technique two to three times a day resets your nervous system.

- **Create a Calm-Down Ritual.**
  Designate a calming ritual at a set time daily—like tea without distractions, a walk in silence, or journaling by candlelight—to give your mind a break from noise and urgency.

- **Eliminate One Source of Daily Overstimulation.**
  Identify and remove a source of chaos (e.g., constant notifications, cluttered desk, loud environments) to create more space for calm in your surroundings.

- **Respond, Don't React.**
  When faced with a trigger, pause for three seconds before responding. That brief pause builds emotional discipline and anchors you in calm, especially during conflict or pressure.

Beyond the Surface

A common misunderstanding about calm is that it's a constant state of stillness or a complete absence of stress—something you reach when life slows down or distractions vanish.

In reality, calm is often a cultivated mindset, a quiet strength that persists amid chaos, not an escape from it. It's about breathing through challenges, grounding yourself in the present, and choosing focus over frenzy. True calm can coexist with a busy life, deepening through practice, awareness, and letting go of the need for perfection.

WHAT'S ON MY MIND RIGHT NOW?

Calm

Tony D. Thelen

Peace

"Remember what peace there may be in silence ..."

Following the call to move placidly, the "Desiderata" urges us to "remember what peace there may be in silence," a gentle reminder of the restorative power found in stillness. In a world that often equates productivity with noise, this element invites us to rediscover peace through quietude.

Silence is not merely the absence of sound but a sacred space where we can reconnect with ourselves, free from distractions. We are made to live peacefully with innate wholeness and resourcefulness.

This timeless wisdom resonates deeply in our hyper-connected age, where constant chatter—whether from devices or our own thoughts—can drown out our inner voice. Sometimes this chatter takes over our lives if we let it, and we need a reminder that we have the power to live peacefully as we deem appropriate.

Peace in silence might be found in a morning moment of solitude, a walk in nature, or simply closing our eyes to breathe. It's in these pauses that we hear the whispers of our intuition, finding clarity and peace. The power is in the pause, not the static and noise around us.

This element teaches us that peace is not a distant ideal but a present possibility, within us, accessible whenever we choose. By honoring moments of silence, we cultivate a deeper sense of tranquility that sustains us through life's storms. We can tap into our own power anytime we need it.

It's a practice of returning to our center, where true peace resides. We've had it all along.

How can you create a moment of silence to rediscover peace today?

BRINGING IT TO LIFE

Peace

- **Limit Daily Exposure to Negativity.**
  Choose a specific time to check the news or social media—then unplug. Protect your mental peace by not allowing constant external noise to hijack your inner state.

- **Embrace Forgiveness, Even Silently.**
  Identify one person you're holding resentment toward and intentionally release that tension—whether or not you speak to them. Forgiveness is less about them and more about your peace.

- **Practice a "Peace Pause" in Conflict.**
  In tense conversations, consciously lower your voice and soften your posture. This disarms escalation and invites a peaceful tone, even in disagreement.

- **Declutter One Area of Your Life.**
  Physical clutter often mirrors mental chaos. Clear one drawer, shelf, or digital folder—it will give your mind a tangible sense of clarity and peace.

- **End Your Day with Gratitude Reflection.**
  Each night, write down three things that brought you peace or joy. This simple practice shifts your mindset toward contentment and anchors you in peaceful awareness.

Beyond the Surface

A common misunderstanding about peace is that it's the total elimination of conflict or noise—something you attain when the world aligns or troubles fade away.

In reality, peace is often an inner refuge, a sense of wholeness that endures despite external storms. It's about accepting what you can't control, finding solace in quiet moments, and fostering compassion for yourself and others. True peace can thrive alongside disagreement, growing through patience, forgiveness, and a steady heart.

WHAT'S ON MY MIND RIGHT NOW?

Peace

Tony D. Thelen

Harmony

*"As far as possible without surrender,
be on good terms with all persons …"*

The "Desiderata" advises us to "be on good terms with all persons, as far as possible without surrender," highlighting the value of harmony in our relationships. This element acknowledges the complexity of human interactions—where differences in values, perspectives, and temperaments can and often do create friction—while urging us to seek connection without compromising our integrity.

Harmony is not about pleasing everyone or sacrificing our principles, but about fostering mutual respect and understanding.

In practice, this might mean listening with an open mind and heart during a disagreement or choosing kindness even when we differ. Ehrmann's wisdom reminds us that relationships thrive on balance, not capitulation.

By striving for harmony, we create a ripple effect of positivity, reducing conflict and building bridges in our communities. This approach also nurtures our own peace, as resentment and strife erode our well-being. In an increasingly polarized world, this element challenges us to rise above divisiveness, finding common ground while staying true to ourselves. Starting with good intentions is a good idea if your goal is harmony.

Harmony becomes a dance of give-and-take, where we honor both our boundaries and the humanity of others. It may not be easy at times, but sometimes important things in life require a little hard work to maintain.

How can you cultivate harmony in a challenging relationship today, without surrendering your core values?

BRINGING IT TO LIFE

Harmony

- **Align Your Schedule with Your Values.**
  Review your calendar for the week. Ask, "Does how I spend my time reflect what matters most to me?" Make one change that brings your actions into alignment with your values.

- **Seek Win-Win Outcomes in Relationships.**
  When disagreements arise, pause and reframe the goal: not "I win" or "you win," but "we both benefit." This mindset creates relational harmony rather than division.

- **Tune In to Your Body's Rhythm.**
  Notice your natural energy cycles throughout the day and honor them. Work during peak focus times and rest or recharge when your body signals the need. Harmony begins within.

- **Curate a Harmonious Environment.**
  Adjust one space in your home or work area to support calm and flow—add music, light a candle, reduce clutter, or introduce nature. Your environment impacts your internal state.

- **Use "Yes, and…" in Conversations.**
  Try to build on others' ideas instead of contradicting them. Look first to see their point of view, then add your thoughts. Be open to other's ways of thinking - it creates conversational harmony, openness, and collaboration.

Beyond the Surface

A common misunderstanding about harmony is that it's everyone agreeing or living in perfect sync—something achieved when differences dissolve or tensions disappear.

In reality, harmony is often the art of blending diverse voices and energies into a cohesive whole, not erasing them. It's about collaboration, mutual respect, and finding rhythm in variety. True harmony can flourish amid diversity, deepening through understanding, compromise, and a shared sense of purpose.

WHAT'S ON MY MIND RIGHT NOW?

Harmony

Tony D. Thelen

Truth

"Speak your truth quietly and clearly ..."

"Speak your truth quietly and clearly," the "Desiderata" instructs, offering a timeless lesson in the power of honest, measured communication. Truth, in this context, is not about harshness or imposition, but about expressing our authentic thoughts and feelings with clarity and calm. We speak, not only our points, but also on why we think the way we do to help others understand us better.

In a world often filled with noise and posturing, this element reminds us that genuine communication doesn't require force—it thrives on sincerity.

Speaking quietly reflects confidence in our truth, free from the need to dominate or shout. Clearly articulating our perspective ensures we're understood, fostering meaningful dialogue. This wisdom is especially relevant in today's headline-driven, soundbite-laden climate, where conversations can quickly escalate into conflict or worse.

By speaking our truth with gentleness, we invite others to listen rather than defend.

Practically, this might mean sharing a difficult opinion with a loved one in a way that's respectful or voicing a concern at work without fear of judgment. It's in these instances where the cost of candor can be quite high, but the cost of silence or deference may be much higher.

Truth, when spoken with care, builds trust and deepens connections. It also liberates us from the burden of pretense, aligning our words with our inner values.

How might you speak and seek your truth today, ensuring your voice is both clear and compassionate?

BRINGING IT TO LIFE

Truth

- **Speak Honestly with Compassion.**

    In at least one interaction each day, choose to express your honest thoughts or feelings—kindly and clearly. Truth without kindness alienates; truth with compassion connects.

- **Do a Daily "Truth Check-In".**

    Take three minutes to ask yourself, "What am I pretending not to know?" Write down any insights. This cultivates inner honesty and helps uncover blind spots.

- **Honor Your Inner Voice Over External Noise.**

    When faced with a decision, pause and ask: What feels right for me—not what others expect? Let your inner wisdom guide your next step, even in small choices.

- **Keep Your Word, Especially to Yourself.**

    Whether it's a commitment to walk, call someone, or stop working by 6 p.m., follow through. Integrity in small actions builds a life grounded in truth.

- **Gently Challenge False Narratives.**

    Notice a limiting belief you carry ("I'm not good at that," "this never works out"). Ask, "Is this really true?" Replace it with something truer and more empowering.

THINGS WE DESIRE

Beyond the Surface

A common misunderstanding about truth is that it's a fixed, obvious fact—something you uncover fully when all doubts are erased, or with evidence that cannot be denied.

In reality, truth is often a layered, evolving understanding, shaped by perspective, experience, and context rather than a single, unchangeable answer. It's about seeking clarity with an open mind, embracing ambiguity, and valuing honesty over certainty. Absolute truth can evolve through reflection, dialogue, and humility, and even ambiguity.

WHAT'S ON MY MIND RIGHT NOW?

Truth

Tony D. Thelen

Listen

*"Listen to others, even the dull and the ignorant;
they too have their story …"*

The "Desiderata" encourages us to "listen to others, even the dull and the ignorant; they too have their story," emphasizing the transformative power of listening. This element challenges our tendency to dismiss those we deem uninteresting or uninformed, reminding us that every person carries a unique narrative shaped by their experiences. Every human life is valuable, and worthy of respect.

True listening goes beyond hearing words—it's an act of empathy, a willingness to understand another's perspective, no matter how different from our own. In a fast-paced world, where we often prioritize speaking over hearing, this wisdom invites us to slow down and be present. Hear not only the words being spoken, but the tone of the voice, and the circumstances around the person and the message. Listen holistically to understand, not to be understood.

Listening to someone we might otherwise overlook—like a quiet coworker or a struggling neighbor—can reveal unexpected insights and foster connection. It teaches humility, as we recognize that wisdom can emerge from unlikely sources. You may be the only person who notices a person during a time of need, simply because you chose to listen instead of ignore.

Practically, this might involve setting aside distractions to fully engage in a conversation, or asking questions to draw out someone's story.

By listening, we honor the inherent worth of others, creating space for mutual respect. When we listen to each other, we enlarge the world and our time in it.

This element reminds us that understanding is the foundation of compassion, bridging divides and enriching our lives.

Who might you listen to today with fresh ears?

BRINGING IT TO LIFE

Listen

- **Pause Before You Respond.**

    In conversations, build a two to three second pause before replying. This simple act shows respect, prevents interruption, and ensures you're truly hearing—not just reacting.

- **Listen Without Fixing.**

    The next time someone shares a problem, resist the urge to solve it. Instead, reflect back what you heard. Often, people seek understanding more than advice.

- **Eliminate Distractions During Conversations.**

    When someone is speaking, silence your phone, close your laptop, or turn away from the screen. Show with your body language that your attention is undivided.

- **Ask One Deeper Question.**

    In your next meaningful conversation, ask a follow-up like "What makes you feel that way?" or "Can you tell me more?" Deep listening invites deeper connection.

▪ **Listen to Yourself Once a Day.**

Spend five quiet minutes alone, without input or distraction. Tune in to what your body, mind, or heart is saying. Self-listening is the foundation of listening to others well.

Beyond the Surface

A common misunderstanding about listening is that it's just passively hearing words—something you do when someone talks, expecting to respond or solve problems.

In reality, listening is an active, empathetic engagement, a way of truly hearing someone's heart and story, not just their voice. It's about being present, suspending judgment, and connecting deeply. True listening can occur amid distractions, deepening through patience, curiosity, and a willingness to learn.

WHAT'S ON MY MIND RIGHT NOW?

Listen

Tony D. Thelen

Serenity

*"Avoid loud and aggressive persons,
they are vexations to the spirit …"*

In the "Desiderata", the counsel to "avoid loud and aggressive persons, they are vexations to the spirit" serves as a reminder to protect our serenity. This element highlights the impact of our environment on our inner peace, cautioning against those whose volatility disrupts our calm.

Loudness and aggression—whether in words, actions, or energy—can drain our spirit, leaving us unsettled and reactive. Ehrmann's wisdom encourages us to set boundaries, choosing to distance ourselves from negativity that threatens our well-being.

This isn't about judgment, but self-preservation, recognizing that serenity is a precious state worth safeguarding. The state of being "untroubled" has its own rewards.

In practice, this might mean stepping away from a heated argument, limiting time with a consistently hostile person, or seeking out calmer company. It could mean ending relationships that bring chronic problems to your life. By prioritizing serenity, we create space for clarity and joy, free from the turbulence of others' unrest.

This element also invites us to reflect on our own behavior—do we contribute to peace or discord? In a world often marked by conflict, cultivating serenity becomes an act of strength, allowing us to engage in life from a place of balance and perspective.

How can you protect your serenity today by choosing your surroundings wisely?

> BRINGING IT TO LIFE

Serenity

- **Create a Daily Quiet Space.**

    Set aside ten minutes each day in a calm setting—no agenda, no input. Just sit, breathe, and allow stillness. Serenity often arrives when you stop chasing it.

- **Let Go of What You Can't Control.**

    Write down one thing causing stress that's outside your control. Then, physically release it—tear up the paper, toss it, or say aloud, "This is not mine to carry."

- **Simplify One Area of Your Life.**

    Serenity grows in simplicity. Choose one small area—your inbox, your morning routine, your commitments—and remove what's unnecessary or draining.

- **Speak Slowly and Gently.**

    Throughout the day, deliberately slow your speech and lower your tone. This not only calms others, but centers you in serenity, especially in high-stress moments.

- **End Your Day with a Serenity Anchor.**

    Establish a soothing nightly ritual—such as reading something peaceful, lighting a candle, or doing gentle stretches—that signals to your mind, "It is safe to be still."

THINGS WE DESIRE

Beyond the Surface

A common misunderstanding about serenity is that it means living a life completely free of stress, noise, or conflict—as if serenity can only be found in perfect external circumstances like a quiet beach or mountaintop retreat.

In reality, serenity is an internal state of calm acceptance, not the absence of challenge or tension. True serenity is found within, even amid chaos, because it comes from clarity, perspective, and emotional regulation—not from controlling the world around us. It's the ability to remain grounded when life gets loud.

WHAT'S ON MY MIND RIGHT NOW?

Serenity

Tony D. Thelen

Contentment

*"If you compare yourself with others,
you may become vain and bitter ..."*

The "Desiderata" warns, "If you compare yourself with others, you may become vain and bitter," offering a profound lesson in contentment. This element speaks to the human tendency to measure our worth against others, a habit that often leads to feelings of inadequacy or arrogance. If you are the parent of a teenager, you know well the damage of social media and the challenges kids face when it comes to contentment.

Comparison traps us in a cycle of discontent, where we either feel superior and vain or inferior and bitter. It seems to feed on the extremes, with neither serving us well.

Ehrmann's wisdom invites us to break free from this cycle by focusing on our own journey, finding fulfillment in our unique path. Contentment arises when we appreciate our own strengths and progress, rather than looking outward for validation. We keep an internal scorecard, free from superficial labels around us.

In today's social media-driven world, where curated lives fuel comparison, this lesson feels especially urgent, even for adults.

Practically, we might cultivate contentment by celebrating our small victories, practicing gratitude for what we have, or limiting exposure to idealized images. By letting go of comparison, we reclaim our self-worth, rooting it in authenticity rather than external standards.

This element reminds us that true happiness lies in embracing our individuality, free from the distortions of envy or pride. We honor the journey we are on, not the storyboards of Instagram, Facebook, or TikTok.

How can you shift your focus inward today to nurture a deeper sense of contentment?

BRINGING IT TO LIFE

Contentment

- **Practice the "Enough" Mindset.**

    Throughout the day, repeat the quiet affirmation, "This is enough. I am enough." Say it when you eat, work, or rest to gently counter the pull of constant striving.

- **Savor the Present Moment.**

    Once a day, pause and fully engage your senses—feel the warmth of your coffee mug, the sun on your skin, or a kind word from someone. Contentment often hides in the ordinary.

- **Compare Less, Appreciate More.**

    Limit social media use or take a short break entirely. Each time you feel comparison rising, turn inward and list three things you're genuinely grateful for in your life right now.

- **Celebrate Small Wins.**

    Acknowledge daily progress, not just major milestones. Write down one thing you did well or handled gracefully today—this builds inner satisfaction regardless of outcomes.

▪ **Live Within Your Means.**

Make one conscious choice to reduce excess—whether it's spending, consuming, or overcommitting. Simplicity and contentment often walk hand in hand.

Beyond the Surface

A common misunderstanding about contentment is that it's settling for mediocrity or giving up on ambition—something you feel when you stop striving or dreams fade.

In reality, contentment is a rich satisfaction with the now, a balance of gratitude and growth, not stagnation. It's about cherishing what you have while pursuing what matters, finding joy in the journey. True contentment can thrive alongside goals, deepening through appreciation, purpose, and a light-hearted acceptance of life's ebb and flow.

WHAT'S ON MY MIND RIGHT NOW?

Contentment

Tony D. Thelen

Acceptance

*"For always there will be greater
and lesser persons than yourself..."*

The "Desiderata" continues its reflection on comparison with the insight, "for always there will be greater and lesser persons than yourself," a call to embrace acceptance. This element grounds us in the reality of human diversity—there will always be others who surpass us in talent, success, or status, just as there will be those we surpass. We all come from different starting places, and accepting ourselves for who we are is honorable in and of itself.

Rather than fueling insecurity or superiority, this truth invites us to accept our place in the spectrum of humanity with humility.

Acceptance here means releasing the need to rank ourselves, instead valuing our unique contributions while honoring others. In a competitive world, this wisdom offers relief, reminding us that our worth isn't tied to being the best, but to being our best selves. The greatest of all coaches in sports never look at the scoreboard, but only ask that their players give their very best, in practice and in games. If they did this, they had already won in the coach's mind.

Practically, we might practice acceptance by reframing feelings of envy as inspiration, or mentoring someone less experienced without judgment.

This element fosters peace by dissolving the pressure to constantly prove ourselves. It encourages a mindset of coexistence, where we celebrate others' successes without diminishing our own. By accepting the natural hierarchy of abilities, we find freedom to grow at our own pace and to be ourselves.

How can you embrace acceptance today, honoring both your strengths and limitations?

BRINGING IT TO LIFE

Acceptance

- **Acknowledge What Is—Without Judgment.**

  When something frustrates you, name it without trying to change or resist it. Say, "This is what's happening right now." Acceptance begins with honest recognition.

- **Practice Self-Acceptance Through Kind Self-Talk.**

  Replace harsh inner dialogue with compassionate phrases like, "I'm doing the best I can" or "It's okay to be learning." Speak to yourself the way you would a dear friend.

- **Release One "Should" Today.**

  Notice where you're holding yourself—or others—to an unrealistic standard. Choose one "I should …" or "They should …" to let go of, and observe how your peace expands.

- **Sit with Discomfort Instead of Resisting It.**

  The next time you feel emotional discomfort (e.g., sadness, fear, irritation), allow yourself to feel it for ninety seconds without distraction. This creates space for acceptance to unfold.

- **Extend Grace to Others.**
When someone makes a mistake or falls short of your expectations, pause before reacting. Say internally, "They're human, just like me." Acceptance builds relational peace.

Beyond the Surface

A common misunderstanding about acceptance is that it's a passive surrender or giving up—something you feel when you stop fighting or resign yourself to a bad situation.

In reality, acceptance is an active, empowering choice, a recognition of what is while opening the door to peace and growth, not defeat. It's about embracing reality with clarity, releasing resistance, and finding strength in moving forward. True acceptance can coexist with change, deepening through courage, self-compassion, and a willingness to let go of what no longer serves you.

WHAT'S ON MY MIND RIGHT NOW?

Acceptance

Tony D. Thelen

Joy

"Enjoy your achievements as well as your plans ..."

"Enjoy your achievements as well as your plans," the "Desiderata" advises, illuminating the importance of joy in both our past successes and future aspirations. This element reminds us to pause and savor what we've accomplished, rather than always rushing toward the next goal.

In a culture that often glorifies relentless ambition, this wisdom invites balance—celebrating the present while dreaming of the future. Joy in our achievements might mean reflecting on a project completed, a skill mastered, or a relationship nurtured, allowing ourselves to feel pride without guilt. Equally, finding joy in our plans keeps us inspired, infusing our goals with hope, inspiration, and excitement.

Practically, we might take a moment to journal about a recent success or share our dreams with a friend to amplify their joy. This element teaches us that happiness is not deferred to some distant milestone but woven into every step of our journey. Happiness IS the journey.

By embracing joy in both what we've done and what lies ahead, we cultivate a life of fulfillment, where gratitude and anticipation coexist. This balance fuels our motivation while grounding us in the present.

How can you find joy today in both your achievements and your plans?

> BRINGING IT TO LIFE

Joy

- **Create a "Joy List" and Do One Thing from It Daily.**

   Write down ten small things that reliably bring you joy, like dancing to music, calling a friend, or being in nature. Pick one each day and intentionally make time for it.

- **Celebrate Something–Anything–Each Day.**

   Pause at least once to acknowledge something good: a finished task, a kind word, or simply the chance to breathe and begin again. Joy often comes in moments we choose to notice.

- **Surround Yourself with Uplifting Inputs.**

   Start your morning with something joyful—play a favorite song, read something that lifts you, or look at a photo that makes you smile. Input shapes mindset.

- **Be Fully Present in a Moment of Delight.**

   When joy shows up—however small—don't rush past it. Linger. Let yourself feel it fully, without guilt or distraction. Presence magnifies joy.

- **Give Joy Freely to Someone Else.**

   Do one unexpected act of kindness: compliment a stranger, send a funny message, or leave a small note of encouragement. Joy multiplies when shared.

THINGS WE DESIRE

Beyond the Surface

Joy is not a fleeting emotion dependent on external events, something you feel only when everything is going well or when you're celebrating a major success.

Joy is a deeper, more enduring state that can exist even alongside difficulty or sorrow. It's often found in small, quiet moments—connection with others, gratitude, purpose, or simply being present. Unlike momentary happiness, joy is less about what happens to you and more about how you choose to engage with life.

WHAT'S ON MY MIND RIGHT NOW?

Joy

Tony D. Thelen

Purpose

"Keep interested in your own career, however humble …"

The "Desiderata" encourages us to "keep interested in your own career, however humble," a reminder to find purpose in our work, regardless of its scale or recognition. This element challenges societal biases that equate worth with prestige, and instead affirms the dignity of all labor.

Purpose arises not from external validation but from our engagement with what we do—whether we're a teacher, a gardener, a caregiver, or provide any number of labor services. Staying interested means approaching our work with curiosity, seeking growth and meaning even in mundane and routine tasks.

In a world that often pushes us to chase bigger titles or salaries, this wisdom invites us to find fulfillment in the present, valuing the impact we make, however small.

Practically, we might rekindle purpose by learning a new skill within our role, or reflecting on how our work serves others. This element reminds us that every job, when approached with intention, becomes a vessel for personal growth and contribution.

By staying engaged, we anchor ourselves in a sense of purpose that transcends external measures of success. This fosters resilience, as our work becomes a source of meaning, not just a means to an end.

How can you rediscover purpose in your career today?

BRINGING IT TO LIFE

Purpose

- **Start Your Day by Asking "What Matters Most Today"?**

  Before diving into tasks, identify one action that aligns with your deeper values or long-term goals. Let that anchor your priorities for the day.

- **Connect Small Actions to Bigger Meaning.**

  Whether you're making a meal, attending a meeting, or helping a friend, pause and ask, "How does this contribute to something larger than me?" Purpose is often found in the ordinary.

- **Review Your "Why" Weekly.**

  Take ten minutes each week to journal or reflect on your personal mission—what drives you, inspires you, and gives your work or relationships meaning. Reconnect to your why.

- **Say No to One Thing That Distracts You.**

  Purposeful living requires focus. Choose one activity, habit, or obligation that doesn't align with your purpose—and gently release it or say no.

- **Encourage Purpose in Others.**

  Ask someone what lights them up, or remind them of their strengths and impact. Helping others rediscover purpose can deepen your own sense of it.

THINGS WE DESIRE

Beyond the Surface

Purpose is not something you have to "find" once and for all—like a hidden treasure or single calling that defines your entire life.

Purpose is something you cultivate over time, and it can evolve through different seasons of life. It's not always one big thing; it often emerges from how you live rather than what you do. Purpose can be shaped through service, curiosity, connection, or commitment—and it often grows clearer as you engage with life, not just when you try to figure it out in advance.

WHAT'S ON MY MIND RIGHT NOW?

Purpose

_____
_____
_____
_____
_____
_____
_____
_____
_____
_____

Tony D. Thelen

Stability

"It is a real possession in the changing fortunes of time ..."

Referring to our career, the "Desiderata" notes, "it is a real possession in the changing fortunes of time," highlighting the stability that meaningful work provides. This element underscores the enduring value of our efforts, even as life's circumstances shift—whether through economic downturns, personal upheavals, or societal changes.

Our career, when rooted in purpose and engagement, becomes a steady anchor, offering a sense of continuity amidst uncertainty. Stability here is not about rigidity, but about the grounding force of having something to return to, a craft or role that we've cultivated over time.

In a world where change is constant, this wisdom reminds us that our skills, experiences, and contributions are lasting possessions that no external force can take away.

Practically, we might nurture this stability by documenting our professional growth, or revisiting the core values that drew us to our work. This element encourages us to see our career as a source of resilience, a foundation we can lean on when other aspects of life feel unsteady.

By valuing our work as a "real possession," we find confidence in our ability to weather life's storms.

How can your career provide stability for you today?

BRINGING IT TO LIFE

Stability

- **Stick to a Consistent Morning Routine.**

    Begin each day with the same two to three foundational activities, like stretching, journaling, or a quiet cup of coffee. A stable morning rhythm creates calm and predictability.

- **Track One Key Habit Daily.**

    Choose a habit that anchors you (e.g., sleep, movement, hydration, prayer) and track it for accountability. Consistency in small things builds long-term stability.

- **Limit Reactive Decisions.**

    When faced with a sudden choice or emotion, pause for ten seconds and ask, "Is this aligned with who I want to be?" Stability comes from thoughtful—not impulsive—action.

- **Review Finances Briefly Each Week.**

    Set a fifteen-minute appointment once a week to look over your spending, saving, or upcoming bills. Financial awareness, even in small doses, contributes to life stability.

- **Protect Your Boundaries.**

    Say "no" or "not right now" to one commitment that overstretches you. Stability often means honoring your limits so you can stay grounded and resilient.

Beyond the Surface

Stability doesn't mean that everything stays the same—that life is predictable, unchanging, and under control.

Stability is not the absence of change, but the ability to remain centered and resilient amid change. It's an inner steadiness that allows you to adapt without falling apart. True stability comes from strong values, supportive relationships, and healthy habits—not from trying to freeze life in place. It's about building a solid foundation, not resisting the inevitable movement of life.

WHAT'S ON MY MIND RIGHT NOW?

Stability

Tony D. Thelen

Prudence

"Exercise caution in your business affairs ..."

The "Desiderata" advises us to "exercise caution in your business affairs," a timeless call to practice prudence in our decisions. This element speaks to the importance of careful thought and foresight, especially in matters of finance, work, or partnerships, where impulsivity can lead to regret.

Prudence involves weighing risks, seeking advice, and considering long-term consequences rather than chasing short-term gains. In today's fast-paced world, where trends and opportunities can tempt hasty choices, this wisdom urges us to slow down and act with intention.

Practically, exercising caution might mean reviewing a contract thoroughly, saving before spending, or researching a business venture before committing—seemingly basic activities, but at times in our chaotic lives, we tend to overlook them.

This element reminds us that prudence is not about fear, but about wisdom—protecting our resources and relationships from unnecessary harm. By making thoughtful decisions, we build a foundation of trust and reliability, both with others and within ourselves.

Ehrmann's counsel encourages a balanced approach, where we pursue opportunities with clarity rather than recklessness. Prudence becomes a shield, safeguarding our stability while allowing us to grow.

In a world that often glorifies speed, this element invites us to value deliberation as a path to lasting success.

How can you practice prudence in a decision today?

BRINGING IT TO LIFE

Prudence

- **Pause Before Making Decisions.**

  Before saying "yes" or "no" to a request or impulse, take a short pause to ask yourself, "What are the long-term consequences of this?" Prudence lives in that moment of reflection.

- **Use the "Next Right Step" Filter.**

  Instead of chasing perfection, ask, "What's the next wise step I can take today?" This keeps you moving forward with care, not fear or urgency.

- **Seek Counsel Before Major Choices.**

  When facing an important decision, reach out to a trusted advisor, mentor, or friend. Prudence is not about isolation—it's about drawing from wisdom beyond your own.

- **Limit Emotion-Driven Reactions.**

  Notice moments when strong emotions push you to act quickly. Write down the feeling, then wait before responding. Prudence respects emotion, but isn't ruled by it.

- **Keep a Decision Journal.**

  At the end of each day, reflect on one choice you made and what you learned from it. Over time, this sharpens your judgment and helps pattern more deliberate decision-making.

Beyond the Surface

Prudence is not simply being cautious or risk-averse, avoiding bold moves or playing it safe out of fear.

Prudence is the practice of wise decision-making, grounded in foresight, reflection, and good judgment. It's not about avoiding action—it's about taking thoughtful action. Prudence balances courage with discernment, allowing you to weigh consequences, stay aligned with your values, and act with integrity even in complex situations. It's less about fear and more about intentionality.

WHAT'S ON MY MIND RIGHT NOW?

Prudence

Tony D. Thelen

Awareness

"For the world is full of trickery..."

The "Desiderata" warns, "for the world is full of trickery," urging us to cultivate awareness as we navigate life's complexities. This element acknowledges the reality of deception—whether in business, relationships, or societal systems—where hidden agendas or false promises can lead us astray.

Awareness becomes our defense; a heightened sense of discernment that helps us see through illusions and protect our well-being. In a digital age rife with misinformation, scams, and superficiality, this wisdom feels especially relevant. It encourages us to question, research, and trust our instincts rather than accepting things at face value.

Practically, we might develop awareness by staying informed, seeking multiple perspectives, or pausing to reflect before acting. This element doesn't advocate cynicism, but rather a clear-eyed approach to reality, where we remain open-hearted yet vigilant. By staying aware, we safeguard our resources, time, and trust, ensuring they're invested in what's genuine.

Ehrmann's counsel reminds us that awareness empowers us to move through the world with confidence, unswayed by trickery. It's a call to balance openness with caution, so we can engage with life fully without being blindsided.

How can you sharpen your awareness today?

> **BRINGING IT TO LIFE**

Awareness

- **Do a Three-Minute Body Scan Each Morning.**

  Before checking your phone or starting tasks, close your eyes and mentally scan your body from head to toe. This grounds you in the present and heightens physical and emotional awareness.

- **Name What You're Feeling—Without Judgment.**

  At least once during the day, pause and ask, "What am I feeling right now?" Label the emotion (e.g., "irritated," "hopeful," "anxious") without trying to fix or change it.

- **Observe, Don't Absorb.**

  When you're in a chaotic or tense environment, mentally note what's happening ("She's frustrated," "There's tension in the room") while staying centered in your own calm. This builds situational awareness without losing emotional stability.

- **Practice One Act of Mindful Noticing.**

  Pick an ordinary activity—eating, walking, or listening—and give it your full attention. Notice details: textures, sounds, and emotions. Mindful noticing sharpens moment-to-moment awareness.

- **Reflect on One Insight Each Evening.**

  At the end of your day, ask: "What did I notice today that I might have missed if I wasn't paying attention?" This reinforces a habit of awareness and presence.

Beyond the Surface

A common misunderstanding about awareness is that it's purely intellectual—just knowing facts, being observant, or paying attention to your surroundings.

In truth, awareness is a deeper, more integrated state of being fully present, where you notice not only what's happening around you, but also what's happening within you—your thoughts, emotions, biases, and patterns. True awareness invites reflection without judgment and creates space for wiser choices. It's not just about seeing clearly; it's about seeing with openness, humility, and intention.

WHAT'S ON MY MIND RIGHT NOW?

Awareness

Tony D. Thelen

Virtue

"But let this not blind you to what virtue there is …"

Despite the world's trickery, "Desiderata" advises, "but let this not blind you to what virtue there is," a reminder to seek and honor virtue amidst life's challenges. This element encourages us to look beyond deception and focus on the goodness that exists—acts of kindness, integrity, and compassion that illuminate the human spirit.

Virtue is the moral compass that guides us, a quality we can both embody and recognize in others. In a world where negativity often dominates, this wisdom invites us to shift our gaze, noticing the quiet heroism of those who act with honor, often away from the headlines.

We might cultivate virtue by practicing honesty in our dealings, or by acknowledging someone's good deed with gratitude. This element teaches us that focusing on virtue doesn't mean ignoring reality—it means choosing to amplify what's right and true. By doing so, we inspire others to act virtuously, creating a ripple effect of positivity.

Ehrmann's counsel reminds us that virtue is a beacon, guiding us toward a life of meaning and connection. It's a call to remain hopeful, seeing the best in humanity while navigating its flaws.

How can you honor virtue in your actions today?

BRINGING IT TO LIFE

Virtue

- **Choose One Virtue to Practice Intentionally Today.**

    Each morning, select a virtue—like patience, humility, courage, or kindness—and carry it with you as a quiet compass. Ask, "How can I live this out in my choices today?"

- **Do the Right Thing, Even When It's Inconvenient.**

    Look for one moment to act with integrity, especially when no one is watching. Virtue is built not by grand gestures, but by steady, unseen choices.

- **Own a Mistake Without Excuse.**

    When you fall short, admit it clearly and humbly. Growth in virtue includes self-honesty and a willingness to make amends, not perform perfection.

- **Honor Someone Else's Virtue Out Loud.**

    Each day, affirm someone for a virtue they've demonstrated—like loyalty, compassion, or diligence. Noticing virtue in others reinforces your own.

- **Reflect on Your Character, Not Just Your Results.**

    At day's end, ask, "Was I the kind of person I want to be today?" Track progress in who you're becoming—not just what you're accomplishing.

Beyond the Surface

A common misunderstanding about virtue is that it's about moral perfection or rigid adherence to rules—being flawless, self-righteous, or superior to others.

In reality, virtue is about striving to live with integrity, humility, and consistency of character, even when no one is watching. It's not about being perfect—it's about being intentional. True virtue is expressed through everyday actions: honesty in hard conversations, kindness under stress, and courage in uncertainty. It's a lifelong practice of aligning who you are with what you believe is right.

WHAT'S ON MY MIND RIGHT NOW?

Virtue

Tony D. Thelen

Aspiration

"Many persons strive for high ideals …"

The "Desiderata" observes, "many persons strive for high ideals," celebrating the human capacity for aspiration. This element highlights the beauty of our drive to reach beyond the ordinary, pursuing goals that reflect our deepest values—whether justice, creativity, or service.

Aspiration fuels our motivation, giving us a sense of purpose and direction. In a world that can feel cynical, this wisdom reminds us that countless individuals are quietly working toward noble causes, from advocating for equality to innovating for a better future. Their efforts inspire us to set our own high ideals, aligning our actions with what matters most.

Practically, we might nurture aspiration by setting a meaningful goal, or supporting someone else's dream with encouragement. This element encourages us to dream big while staying grounded in integrity, ensuring our aspirations uplift rather than divide.

Ehrmann's words affirm that striving for high ideals is a universal trait, connecting us through shared hopes. By embracing aspiration, we tap into our potential, contributing to a world where ideals like compassion and truth can flourish. This pursuit becomes a source of inspiration, reminding us of our capacity for greatness.

What high ideal can you aspire to today?

BRINGING IT TO LIFE

Aspiration

- **Visualize the Future You Want—Daily.**

  Spend two to three minutes each morning picturing your aspirational life with clarity. See yourself living it. This keeps your dreams emotionally alive and mentally focused.

- **Set One Stretch Goal Per Week.**

  Choose one small but meaningful action that nudges you beyond your comfort zone. Aspirations grow when you consistently take bold, imperfect steps forward.

- **Surround Yourself with Uplifting Voices.**

  Read, listen to, or speak with people who inspire you—authors, mentors, or peers. Aspiration thrives in the company of vision and encouragement.

- **Write Down One Reason Why You're Reaching Higher.**

  Clarify your "why" in a sentence or two. Review it often. Keeping your aspirations rooted in purpose helps sustain effort when motivation fades.

- **Track Progress, Not Perfection.**

  Each evening, note one thing you did that aligns with your aspirations—no matter how small. Celebrating progress builds momentum and belief.

Beyond the Surface

A common misunderstanding about aspiration is that it's just ambition dressed up—focused on achievement, status, or climbing the ladder of success.

In truth, aspiration is a deeper inner drive to grow, become, and contribute to something meaningful. It's less about external rewards and more about becoming the fullest version of yourself. True aspiration is rooted in purpose, not ego—it's the quiet fire that keeps you learning, stretching, and striving not just for more, but for better. It asks not just "What can I get?" but "Who can I become?"

WHAT'S ON MY MIND RIGHT NOW?

Aspiration

Tony D. Thelen

Courage

"Everywhere life is full of heroism…"

"Everywhere life is full of heroism," the "Desiderata" declares, a powerful acknowledgment of the courage that surrounds us. This element invites us to see the extraordinary in the ordinary—the everyday acts of bravery that often go unnoticed. Heroism isn't limited to grand gestures; it's in the parent who perseveres through hardship, the friend who speaks up against injustice, or the stranger who offers kindness in a moment of need.

Courage manifests in facing fears, standing firm in our values, or simply continuing on despite adversity. In a world that can feel daunting, this wisdom inspires us to recognize and draw strength from the bravery around us.

We might cultivate courage by taking a small risk, like voicing an unpopular opinion, or by honoring someone else's heroic act with gratitude. This element reminds us that courage is contagious, and witnessing it in others emboldens us to act with bravery ourselves.

Ehrmann's words celebrate the resilience of the human spirit, urging us to see life as a tapestry woven with countless threads of personal, daily heroism. By embracing courage, we contribute to this legacy, adding our own acts of bravery to the whole.

Where can you find or show courage today?

BRINGING IT TO LIFE
Courage

- **Do One Thing That Scares You (Slightly).**
  Choose a small action that stretches you—a tough conversation, a bold ask, or sharing your true opinion. Courage isn't absence of fear, but movement through it.

- **Speak Your Truth with Respect.**
  Find one opportunity each day to express your honest thoughts, even if your voice shakes. Courage is strengthened every time you choose authenticity over approval.

- **Take Imperfect Action Toward a Goal.**
  Don't wait until it's perfect—just begin. Making progress despite uncertainty is a hallmark of courage. Forward movement builds confidence.

- **Remind Yourself of Past Brave Moments.**
  At day's end, reflect on one time in your life when you showed courage. Let that memory fuel today's resolve to act with boldness again.

- **Support Someone Else's Courage.**
  Encourage someone who's stepping into a challenge. Remind them—and yourself—that courage is contagious and grows in connection.

Beyond the Surface

A common misunderstanding about courage is that it means being fearless—charging ahead without doubt, hesitation, or vulnerability.

In reality, courage is not the absence of fear, but the decision to move forward despite it. It often looks quiet and uncertain—not loud or heroic. Courage is speaking the truth when it's uncomfortable, making a change when the outcome isn't guaranteed, or standing alone when it's easier to go along. It's about honoring your values, even when it costs you something. Real courage feels shaky, not invincible—and that's what makes it brave in the first place.

WHAT'S ON MY MIND RIGHT NOW?

Courage

Tony D. Thelen

Authenticity

"Be yourself..."

"Be yourself," the "Desiderata" urges, a simple yet profound call to authenticity. This element cuts through the pressures of conformity, reminding us that our true value lies in our uniqueness. In a world that often demands we fit in—whether through social norms, trends, or expectations—authenticity becomes an act of courage. It means honoring our values, passions, and quirks, even when they differ from the crowd.

Being ourselves allows us to live with integrity, free from the exhaustion of pretense. This wisdom resonates deeply in an age of curated personas, where social media can tempt us to present a false self.

Practically, we might embrace authenticity by expressing a genuine opinion, pursuing a hobby we love, or setting boundaries that reflect our needs. This element teaches us that authenticity fosters deeper connections, as others are drawn to our realness. It also liberates us to grow in alignment with our true nature, rather than someone else's ideals.

Ehrmann's counsel reminds us that our individuality is a gift, one that enriches both our lives and the world. By being ourselves, we inspire others to do the same.

How can you embrace authenticity today?

BRINGING IT TO LIFE

Authenticity

- **Check In: "Am I Being True to Myself Right Now"?**

    Pause once or twice during the day and ask this simple question. If the answer is no, adjust your words, actions, or environment to better reflect your true self.

- **Express a Real Thought or Feeling—Even if It's Vulnerable.**

    Choose one moment to share what you actually feel or believe, not what's expected. Authenticity is built through honest, aligned expression.

- **Wear or Do Something That Reflects the Real You.**

    Whether it's your clothing, workspace, or how you greet others—make one visible choice today that feels deeply you. Small cues reinforce inner alignment.

- **Say "No" When You Mean No.**

    Practice honoring your boundaries by declining something that doesn't fit your values or energy. Authenticity often sounds like a respectful "no."

- **Journal Without Filtering.**

    Spend five to ten minutes writing freely about what you're thinking or feeling, without editing for how it "should" sound. This helps you hear and accept your unfiltered truth.

Beyond the Surface

A common misunderstanding about authenticity is that it means saying whatever you feel or you're "just being yourself" without filters, regardless of the impact on others.

In truth, authenticity is about being honest and aligned with your core values, while also being thoughtful and self-aware. It's not an excuse for impulsiveness or bluntness—it's a commitment to integrity. True authenticity balances transparency with empathy, allowing you to show up genuinely while still honoring context, relationships, and growth. It's less about raw expression and more about congruent, intentional living.

WHAT'S ON MY MIND RIGHT NOW?

Authenticity

Tony D. Thelen

Sincerity

"Especially, do not feign affection ..."

"Desiderata" advises, "especially, do not feign affection," emphasizing the importance of sincerity in our relationships. This element warns against the temptation to pretend we care—whether out of obligation, fear of conflict, or a desire to please.

Feigning affection erodes trust, creating a hollow connection that ultimately leaves both parties unfulfilled. Sincerity, on the other hand, builds bonds rooted in truth, where our love and care are genuine. This wisdom challenges us to examine our motives, ensuring our actions reflect our true feelings. In a world where superficial interactions are common, this element invites us to prioritize depth and honesty.

Practically, we might practice sincerity by expressing gratitude only when we truly feel it, or gently declining a commitment we can't authentically support. This approach fosters relationships where both parties feel seen and valued for who they are.

Ehrmann's counsel reminds us that insincere affection diminishes our integrity and the quality of our connections. By choosing sincerity, we create space for real intimacy, where vulnerability and trust can flourish. This element encourages us to lead with our hearts, offering affection that's true and unwavering.

How can you show sincere affection today?

> BRINGING IT TO LIFE

Sincerity

- **Say What You Mean–Kindly and Clearly.**

   In at least one interaction today, speak with heartfelt honesty. Whether it's encouragement, concern, or gratitude, let your words reflect genuine intention.

- **Give a Compliment That Comes from the Heart.**

   Notice something admirable about someone and express it with no agenda. Sincere praise uplifts others and strengthens authentic connection.

- **Avoid Flattery or Pretense.**

   Catch yourself before you say something just to please or impress. Choose instead to speak with respect and truth, even if it's simpler or quieter.

- **Reflect on Your Motives.**

   Before making a decision or offering advice, ask, "Am I doing this for the right reasons?" Aligning your actions with your values builds a foundation of sincerity.

- **Follow Through on What You Promise.**

   Keep your word—even in the small things. Sincerity shows not just in what we say, but in what we do afterward.

Beyond the Surface

A common misunderstanding about sincerity is that it simply means being nice, agreeable, or emotionally expressive.

In reality, sincerity is about being genuine in your intentions, words, and actions, even when it's difficult or unpopular. It's not about pleasing others—it's about showing up with honesty and clarity, free of pretense or manipulation. True sincerity may be quiet or bold, but it's always rooted in truthfulness and care. It's the courage to mean what you say, and the humility to let your actions reflect your heart.

WHAT'S ON MY MIND RIGHT NOW?

Sincerity

Tony D. Thelen

Love

"Neither be cynical about love ..."

"Neither be cynical about love," Ehrmann's "Desiderata" urges, a gentle nudge to keep our hearts open despite life's challenges. This element acknowledges the pain that can accompany love—heartbreak, betrayal, or loss—yet encourages us not to let these experiences harden us.

Cynicism about love can lead us to close off, fearing vulnerability and missing out on one of life's greatest gifts. Ehrmann's wisdom reminds us that love, in all its forms—romantic, familial, or platonic—is worth believing in. It's the force that connects us, heals us, and gives life meaning. In a world where distrust can feel like a safe default, this element invites us to choose hope instead.

Practically, we might nurture love by forgiving a past hurt, expressing appreciation to a loved one, or opening ourselves to new relationships. This approach keeps our capacity for love alive, allowing us to experience its joy and depth.

By rejecting cynicism, we affirm love's transformative power, even in the face of setbacks. Ehrmann's words encourage us to see love as a renewable force, one that thrives when we approach it with faith and openness.

How can you embrace love today, free from cynicism?

> BRINGING IT TO LIFE

Love

- **Offer Undivided Attention to Someone You Care About.**

    Put away distractions and be fully present with someone—listen without rushing, make eye contact, and let them feel seen. Love begins with presence.

- **Express Love Through Words—Don't Assume They Know.**

    Say "I love you," "I appreciate you," or "I'm proud of you" to someone who needs to hear it. Unspoken love often goes unfelt.

- **Do One Selfless Act with No Expectation.**

    Whether it's a kind gesture, a note, or a favor, give love freely—without needing anything in return. True love is generous, not transactional.

- **Extend Love to Yourself..**

    Speak kindly to yourself today. Forgive a mistake, meet a need, or simply rest. Self-love is the foundation from which all other love flows.

- **Choose Patience in a Moment of Irritation.**

    When someone tests your limits, pause and respond with calm rather than reactivity. Love is often strongest when it's least convenient.

Beyond the Surface

A common misunderstanding about love is that it's just a feeling—romantic, emotional, and effortless when it's "real."

In reality, love is as much a choice and a practice as it is an emotion. It's not always easy or spontaneous; it requires presence, patience, forgiveness, and commitment. True love extends beyond attraction or sentiment—it shows up in action: listening when it's hard, staying when it's inconvenient, and caring when nothing is expected in return. Love isn't just something you feel; it's something you do, again and again.

WHAT'S ON MY MIND RIGHT NOW?

Love

Tony D. Thelen

Hope

"For in the face of all aridity and disenchantment it is as perennial as the grass …"

Speaking of love, "Desiderata" affirms, "for in the face of all aridity and disenchantment it is as perennial as the grass," a beautiful testament to hope.

This element acknowledges life's inevitable dry spells—moments of emotional barrenness or disillusionment—yet reminds us that love endures, resilient and evergreen. Like grass that regrows after drought, love persists through hardship, offering a source of renewal.

This wisdom invites us to hold onto hope, trusting in love's ability to flourish even in the toughest times. In a world where despair can feel overwhelming, this element encourages us to look for signs of love's persistence—whether in a kind gesture, a shared smile, or a memory of connection.

Practically, we might cultivate hope by reflecting on past moments when love surprised us with its strength, or by reaching out to someone we care about. This approach keeps our hearts buoyant, reminding us that no season of disenchantment is permanent.

Ehrmann's metaphor of grass teaches us that hope in love is a natural, enduring force, one that can sustain us through life's challenges. By clinging to hope, we ensure love's vitality in our lives.

How can you find hope in love today?

BRINGING IT TO LIFE

Hope

- **Begin the Day with an Uplifting Intention.**

  Each morning, set a hopeful tone by writing or saying, "Something good is possible today." A hopeful mindset opens your eyes to new possibilities.

- **Look for Evidence of Progress.**

  Even in challenging times, notice one area—however small—where growth is happening. Hope builds when you recognize that movement is still occurring.

- **Speak Hope Into Someone Else's Life.**

  Encourage someone who feels stuck or discouraged. A sincere word like "I believe in you" or "You're not alone" can rekindle hope—for both of you.

- **Reconnect to a Bigger Vision.**

  Reflect on what you're working toward, even if it feels far away. Write down why it still matters. Hope often lives in remembering why we keep going.

- **Limit Voices That Drain Your Outlook.**

  Be mindful of what you consume—news, conversations, or social media. Choose at least one hopeful input each day (a podcast, story, quote) to nourish a forward-looking spirit.

Beyond the Surface

A common misunderstanding about hope is that it's passive—just wishful thinking or blind optimism that things will somehow get better without effort.

In truth, hope is an active, resilient force that fuels perseverance in the face of uncertainty. It's not about denying reality or ignoring hardship—it's about believing that something better is *possible*, and being willing to work toward it. True hope coexists with struggle; it gives us the strength to endure setbacks, imagine new paths, and keep moving forward. Hope is not naïve—it's courageous.

WHAT'S ON MY MIND RIGHT NOW?

Hope

Tony D. Thelen

Wisdom

"Take kindly the counsel of the years, gracefully surrendering the things of youth …"

"Desiderata" advises, "take kindly the counsel of the years, gracefully surrendering the things of youth," a call to embrace the wisdom that comes with aging.

This element invites us to view the passage of time not as a loss but as a teacher, offering lessons through experience. The "counsel of the years" includes the insights we gain from mistakes, successes, and the natural unfolding of life.

Surrendering the things of youth—whether physical vitality, impulsivity, or naive dreams—doesn't mean defeat; it means making peace with change, allowing maturity to deepen our perspective. In a culture that often glorifies youth, this wisdom reminds us that aging brings gifts of clarity, patience, and self-awareness.

Practically, we might embrace this by reflecting on a lesson learned over time, or by letting go of a youthful habit that no longer serves us. This element encourages us to approach aging with grace, seeing it as a journey toward greater understanding.

By accepting the wisdom of our years, we cultivate a richer, more grounded life, where we can mentor others and live with intention.

How can you honor the wisdom of your years today?

BRINGING IT TO LIFE

Wisdom

- **Pause Before You Decide.**

    Take a breath and ask yourself, "What's the wisest response here—not the fastest or easiest?" Wisdom often comes from slowing down and choosing with discernment.

- **Learn from One Experience Each Day.**

    At the end of the day, reflect on one moment where you gained insight—whether from a mistake, a success, or a conversation. Wisdom is accumulated through reflection, not just time.

- **Seek a Perspective Beyond Your Own.**

    Ask a mentor, read a book, or listen to someone with lived experience different from yours. Wisdom deepens when we step outside our own lens.

- **Apply What You Already Know.**

    Choose one piece of advice, knowledge, or truth you already possess and put it into action. Wisdom isn't just knowing what's right—it's doing it.

- **Speak Less, Listen More.**

    In your next conversation, focus more on understanding than replying. Wisdom often emerges not from speaking, but from truly hearing what's beneath the words.

Beyond the Surface

A common misunderstanding about wisdom is that it's simply about knowledge or intelligence—having all the answers, quoting great thinkers, or being the smartest person in the room.

In reality, wisdom is the ability to apply insight, experience, and discernment to life's complex situations with humility and compassion. It's not just about what you know—it's about how you use what you know. True wisdom often involves listening more than speaking, asking thoughtful questions, and knowing when not to act. It recognizes nuance, embraces uncertainty, and seeks the greater good—not just the clever solution.

WHAT'S ON MY MIND RIGHT NOW?

Wisdom

Tony D. Thelen

Resilience

*"Nurture strength of spirit to shield
you in sudden misfortune ..."*

"Nurture strength of spirit to shield you in sudden misfortune," "Desiderata" counsels us, highlighting the importance of resilience in facing life's unexpected challenges. This element recognizes that misfortune—whether loss, failure, or hardship—can strike without warning, testing our emotional fortitude.

Strength of spirit is the inner resource that helps us endure, adapt, and recover, acting as a shield against despair. Resilience doesn't mean avoiding pain, but cultivating the courage to move through it, trusting in our ability to heal. In a world where uncertainty is inevitable, this wisdom encourages us to build our inner strength proactively.

Practically, we might nurture resilience by practicing self-care, seeking support from loved ones, or reflecting on past challenges we've overcome. This element reminds us that our spirit is a renewable force, capable of withstanding life's storms when tended with care.

By fostering resilience, we ensure we're not shattered by misfortune, but instead emerge stronger, with a deeper appreciation for life's highs and lows. Ehrmann's words inspire us to see challenges as opportunities for growth, reinforcing our capacity to rise again.

How can you nurture your strength of spirit to face life's uncertainties?

> BRINGING IT TO LIFE

Resilience

- **Reframe Setbacks as Setups for Growth.**

  When something goes wrong today, pause and ask, "What is this trying to teach me?" Resilience begins with how you interpret adversity.

- **Start a "Bounce-Back" Journal.**

  Each day, write down one challenge you faced and how you responded. Even small comebacks build emotional muscle and reinforce your capacity to endure.

- **Anchor Yourself in Routine.**

  When life feels uncertain, stick to one consistent habit—like morning exercise, a daily walk, or evening reflection. Structure provides stability in the storm.

- **Speak to Yourself Like a Supportive Coach.**

  When you're struggling, replace self-criticism with words like, "This is tough, but I've handled hard things before." Encouraging inner dialogue fuels resilience.

- **Connect with Someone Who Uplifts You.**

  Reach out to someone who reminds you of your strength or reminds you who you are. Resilience isn't about doing it alone—it's about knowing when to lean on others.

Beyond the Surface

A common misunderstanding about resilience is that it means being tough all the time—pushing through without feeling, never breaking down, or handling everything alone.

In reality, resilience is the capacity to bend without breaking—and to recover, adapt, and grow through difficulty. It's not about being unaffected by hardship, but about facing it honestly and still finding a way forward. True resilience allows space for rest, emotion, and support. It's built not through constant strength, but through reflection, connection, and learning. Resilience isn't about never falling—it's about rising again, each time, a bit wiser.

WHAT'S ON MY MIND RIGHT NOW?

Resilience

Tony D. Thelen

Positivity

"But do not distress yourself with dark imaginings …"

"Desiderata" advises, "but do not distress yourself with dark imaginings," a reminder to cultivate positivity by letting go of unnecessary worry. This element addresses our tendency to dwell on worst-case scenarios, where fear and anxiety can spiral into distress.

Dark imaginings—whether about failure, rejection, or loss—often exaggerate reality, stealing our peace and clouding our perspective. Ehrmann's wisdom encourages us to redirect our focus toward what's real and constructive, choosing positivity over fear. In a world filled with uncertainty, this lesson helps us maintain balance, ensuring our thoughts don't become our own worst enemy.

Practically, we might combat dark imaginings by grounding ourselves in the present, practicing mindfulness, or reframing negative thoughts with hope. This element teaches us that while caution is wise, excessive worry is a burden we can release.

By embracing positivity, we free ourselves to experience joy, creativity, and connection, unencumbered by imagined fears.

Ehrmann's counsel reminds us that our mental energy is precious, best spent on thoughts that uplift rather than diminish us. This shift in mindset fosters resilience, allowing us to face challenges with clarity.

How can you replace dark imaginings with positivity today?

BRINGING IT TO LIFE

Positivity

- **Start the Day with a Positive Prompt.**

  Before diving into your to-do list, ask, "What's one thing I'm looking forward to today?" Focusing on anticipation sets a hopeful tone from the outset.

- **Limit Complaints—Replace with Solutions.**

  Catch yourself when you're about to complain, and instead say, "What can I do about it?" Shifting from grumbling to problem-solving builds a habit of optimistic action.

- **Celebrate Small Wins Out Loud.**

  Take a moment to acknowledge one thing that went well—even if it's minor. Positivity multiplies when you name it and share it.

- **Be the Bright Spot for Someone Else.**

  Offer a smile, a sincere compliment, or an encouraging word to someone today. Positivity given is positivity gained.

- **Bookend the Day with Gratitude.**

  Start and end your day by listing one to three things you're grateful for. Gratitude is the most direct path to sustained positivity.

THINGS WE DESIRE

Beyond the Surface

A common misunderstanding about positivity is that it means always being cheerful, ignoring problems, or pretending everything is fine—even when it's not.

In reality, positivity is the choice to focus on what's possible, meaningful, or good—even in the midst of difficulty. It's not about denial or forced happiness; it's about holding space for hope, gratitude, and constructive action without minimizing pain or challenge. True positivity is grounded, not superficial—it acknowledges reality while still choosing to respond with courage, kindness, and perspective.

WHAT'S ON MY MIND RIGHT NOW?

Positivity

Tony D. Thelen

Compassion

*"Beyond a wholesome discipline,
be gentle with yourself..."*

In its closing wisdom, "Desiderata" advises, "beyond a wholesome discipline, be gentle with yourself," a call to balance self-improvement with compassion. This element acknowledges the value of discipline—setting goals, maintaining habits, and striving for growth—but reminds us not to let it harden into self-criticism.

Being gentle with ourselves means offering the same kindness we'd extend to a friend, especially in moments of failure or struggle. In a world that often demands perfection, this wisdom invites us to embrace our humanity, recognizing that mistakes are part of growth.

Compassion toward ourselves fosters emotional well-being, preventing burnout and self-doubt.

Practically, we might practice this by forgiving a recent misstep, taking time to rest, or speaking to ourselves with encouragement. This element teaches us that true discipline is sustainable only when paired with self-love, ensuring we grow without breaking.

Ehrmann's words remind us that we are worthy of care, even as we strive to better ourselves. By cultivating compassion, we create a nurturing inner environment where we can flourish, resilient and whole. This gentle approach becomes a foundation for a life of balance and peace.

How can you be gentle with yourself today?

> **BRINGING IT TO LIFE**

Compassion

- **Start with Self-Compassion.**

    When you make a mistake or feel overwhelmed, replace self-criticism with kindness. Say to yourself, "It's okay. I'm doing the best I can." Compassion for others starts with compassion for yourself.

- **Notice Who Might Be Struggling Silently.**

    Look beyond the surface in your daily interactions. Offer a kind word, a listening ear, or simply your presence to someone who may need support, even if they don't ask.

- **Ask One Genuine Question—and Listen Fully.**

    Ask someone how they're really doing, and give them space to answer. Compassion often begins with caring enough to truly listen without fixing.

- **Interrupt Judgment with Curiosity.**

    When you find yourself judging someone's actions or attitude, pause and think, "What might they be going through?" Curiosity invites understanding.

- **Do One Kind Thing Without Being Noticed.**

    Hold a door, leave an encouraging note, or pick up something someone dropped. Quiet acts of compassion are often the most powerful.

Beyond the Surface

A common misunderstanding about compassion is that it's soft or weak—just feeling sorry for others, or letting people off the hook.

In reality, compassion is a strong, active force that combines empathy with a desire to help alleviate suffering. It's not about pity or permissiveness—it's about understanding others while also holding boundaries, making hard decisions with care, and showing up when it's uncomfortable. True compassion requires courage, emotional strength, and the willingness to act with both heart and clarity. It's love in motion, not just a feeling.

WHAT'S ON MY MIND RIGHT NOW?

Compassion

Tony D. Thelen

Belonging

"You are a child of the universe no less than the trees and the stars; you have a right to be here ..."

In this celestial affirmation, "Desiderata" reminds us that belonging is not earned—it is inherent. Just as the stars need not prove their right to shine, neither must we justify our place in the world.

The line speaks to the quiet, universal truth that each of us is woven into the fabric of existence with the same dignity and wonder as all of creation. This isn't about fitting in—it's about recognizing that we already do. Belonging is not a transaction; it is a birthright.

In daily life, this truth can get buried under rejection, judgment, or the pressure to prove ourselves. But what if we stopped striving to belong and simply accepted that we do?

We belong in our families, our communities, our friendships, and our workspaces—not because we are perfect, but because we are human. When we honor this, we begin to extend that same grace to others. We create spaces where people feel seen, valued, and safe to be fully themselves.

Where in your life do you need to stop proving—and simply start believing—you already belong?

BRINGING IT TO LIFE

Belonging

- **Start Your Day with Affirmation.**

  Each morning, repeat, "I belong here. I am enough." Let these words be your spiritual anchor before the world tells you otherwise.

- **Recall a Moment You Felt Deeply Seen.**

  Take three minutes to remember a time you felt truly accepted. Let that memory remind you of your worth and reinforce that you are not alone.

- **Practice Belonging Forward.**

  Intentionally welcome someone who may feel left out—at work, at home, or in public. Inclusion is contagious and creates belonging for both giver and receiver.

- **Reclaim a Space Where You've Felt Out of Place.**

  Identify a setting where you've doubted your worth (e.g., meetings, family events). Walk into it next time reminding yourself, "I have a right to be here."

- **Unfollow the Voices That Erode Your Worth.**

  Audit your digital and social media inputs. Unsubscribe from people, pages, or patterns that subtly suggest you're not enough. Belonging starts with what we let in.

Beyond the Surface

A common misunderstanding about belonging is that it means fitting in—adapting yourself to be accepted by others, even if it means hiding who you truly are.

In reality, belonging is about being valued and accepted as you are, not as you pretend to be. It's not about changing yourself to match the group; it's about finding or creating spaces where your true self is seen, respected, and included. True belonging starts with self-acceptance and is sustained by mutual respect, not conformity. It's less about fitting in and more about being real and still being welcome.

WHAT'S ON MY MIND RIGHT NOW?

Belonging

Tony D. Thelen

Trust

"And whether or not it is clear to you, no doubt the universe is unfolding as it should ..."

In this line, "Desiderata" invites us into the quiet strength of trust—not a blind, passive hope, but a grounded belief that even in uncertainty, there is meaning.

Life rarely hands us clarity in the moment. The dots only connect looking back. Trust is the bridge we build in the meantime, a decision to live with courage despite the fog. It doesn't mean we know the path—it means we choose to walk anyway.

Bringing this mindset into daily life requires a shift. We live in a world obsessed with control, outcomes, and certainty. But trust reminds us: not everything is ours to direct. We can plant seeds without seeing the harvest yet.

We can endure detours without labeling them as mistakes. Trust is active patience. It's releasing the need to figure everything out and instead focusing on showing up with integrity, compassion, and consistency—believing these choices matter, even if the results aren't instant.

Where do you need to loosen your grip and begin trusting the process more than the outcome?

BRINGING IT TO LIFE

Trust

- **Write a Letter to Your Future Self.**

  Capture what you hope for and what you're working through. Writing to your future self affirms there is a future worth preparing for—and that growth is unfolding.

- **Practice the "Next Right Step" Mindset.**

  Stop trying to map the entire future. Instead, ask yourself, "What is the next right thing I can do today?" Trust is built in small, consistent steps.

- **Reframe Past Detours as Direction.**

  List three events in your life that didn't go as planned, but ultimately served you. Trust deepens when we recognize life's twists as hidden gifts.

- **Embrace Mystery for One Decision This Week.**

  Choose one situation where you normally seek full control and instead say, "I don't know how this will unfold, but I trust that it will." Let go, just once.

- **Anchor in Daily Affirmations of Trust.**

  Start or end your day with a phrase like, "I don't have to know everything to move forward." Remind yourself that trust is a decision, not a feeling.

Beyond the Surface

A common misunderstanding about trust is that it's something you either give blindly or withhold entirely—an all-or-nothing proposition based purely on others' behavior.

In reality, trust is a dynamic, evolving relationship that involves vulnerability, consistency, and discernment. It's not about being naïve or overly guarded—it's about making wise choices based on experience, communication, and shared intent. True trust is built over time, through small, repeated actions, and can be repaired—but not forced. It's not weakness to trust; it's strength to offer it wisely and to honor it when it's given.

WHAT'S ON MY MIND RIGHT NOW?

Trust

Tony D. Thelen

Reverence

*"Therefore be at peace with God,
whatever you conceive Him to be …"*

In another line of *"Desiderata"*, Ehrmann gently urges us to "be at peace with God, whatever you conceive Him to be," a phrase that invites reverence—not just for others, but for the sacredness of our own being. Reverence is a deep respect, a quiet awe for life, for nature, and for the unseen threads that connect us all.

In today's age of speed and self-promotion, reverence can feel countercultural. It asks us to slow down, to notice the grandeur in the ordinary—a sunrise, an old tree, or the wisdom in a child's question. It invites us to regard others not as obstacles or means to an end, but as fellow travelers worthy of kindness and dignity.

Reverence doesn't require ceremony. It thrives in everyday moments when we listen deeply, speak mindfully, or stand still long enough to witness something beautiful. It's the opposite of entitlement—it's humility paired with wonder.

This element reminds us that when we treat life as sacred, life responds in kind. We carry ourselves with more grace. We act with more compassion. We remember that we are part of something larger.

What might shift if you brought a sense of reverence to your next conversation?

> BRINGING IT TO LIFE

Reverence

- **Begin a Daily Moment of Stillness.**

  Each day, take one to two minutes to pause in silence. No agenda, no words—just a moment to acknowledge the presence of something greater than yourself.

- **Identify Your Personal Sacred Space.**

  Find a place that helps you feel connected—whether it's nature, a quiet room, or a place of worship. Visit it regularly to nourish reverence.

- **Practice Interfaith Curiosity.**

  Engage with a perspective or tradition different from your own—not to change your beliefs, but to deepen your respect for the diversity of the sacred.

- **Create a Reverence Ritual.**

  Light a candle, offer gratitude before meals, or pause before starting your work. Small rituals anchor your day in presence and peace.

- **Treat Every Life as Sacred.**

  Whether it's a stranger, a loved one, or yourself—practice speaking, listening, and acting as though each life holds divine worth. Because it does.

Beyond the Surface

A common misunderstanding about reverence is that it's reserved only for religion, rituals, or formal expressions of awe—something distant, stiff, or confined to sacred spaces.

In reality, reverence is a deep sense of respect and wonder for life itself, present in both grand moments and everyday experiences. It's found in the quiet appreciation of nature, the dignity of others, the mystery of existence, or the stillness within. True reverence isn't about formality—it's about presence. It invites humility, gratitude, and a recognition that some things are worthy of our deepest care and attention.

WHAT'S ON MY MIND RIGHT NOW?

Reverence

Tony D. Thelen

Focus

"And whatever your labors and aspirations, in the noisy confusion of life, keep peace in your soul…"

In this line, "Desiderata" speaks directly to the cluttered reality of modern existence—where ambitions pull us forward and demands pull us apart. Yet amid all this motion, he offers a profound directive: keep peace in your soul.

The key to this inner calm? Focus. Not the rigid kind that blocks out the world, but a gentle, anchoring presence that helps us remember what matters. Focus here is not about intensity—it's about intentionality.

In everyday life, we are constantly at risk of being scattered—by digital noise, social pressure, and internal striving. But when we choose focus, we regain our center.

We learn to say yes with purpose and no with peace. Focus is not only about productivity—it's a spiritual discipline that protects our energy and steers our attention toward the meaningful.

When we cultivate focus, we don't escape the noise—we move through it with clarity and calm.

What deserves more of your full attention—and what have you focused on too much?

> BRINGING IT TO LIFE

Focus

- **Define Your Daily Non-Negotiable.**

  Choose one meaningful activity each day—meditation, journaling, exercise, family time—and protect it fiercely. Let it ground your day.

- **Eliminate One Digital Distraction.**

  Silence a recurring notification, uninstall a distracting app, or create screen-free time blocks. You'll gain mental clarity and emotional space.

- **Begin with "Why" Before "What".**

  Before jumping into a task, pause and ask, "Why does this matter?" Let intention—not urgency—guide your priorities.

- **Practice the 90/20 Rule.**

  Work in focused ninety-minute blocks followed by twenty-minute rests. This rhythm aligns with natural brain cycles and boosts sustained attention.

- **Create a "Not-To-Do" List.**

  List three things you will not spend energy on today. Focus is often preserved not by doing more, but by consciously doing less.

Beyond the Surface

A common misunderstanding about focus is that it simply means intense concentration or single-minded attention—shutting everything out to zero in on one task.

In reality, focus is about intentional alignment—knowing what matters most and directing your time, energy, and attention accordingly. It's not just about working harder or longer—it's about working smarter by filtering distractions, setting boundaries, and choosing what not to pursue. True focus creates clarity and purpose, not tunnel vision. It's less about force and more about discipline with direction.

WHAT'S ON MY MIND RIGHT NOW?

Focus

Tony D. Thelen

Beauty

*"With all its sham, drudgery and broken dreams,
it is still a beautiful world …"*

In this closing line, "Desiderata" acknowledges life's harsh truths—its sham, drudgery, and disappointments—and still, he lifts our eyes to something higher.

Beauty persists not in spite of pain, but often alongside it. This is not a call to deny suffering, but to refuse to let it blind us. To name the world as beautiful, even when it's bruised, is a radical act of hope and perception.

Beauty is not confined to perfect moments or curated images. It lives in the overlooked, the ordinary, the imperfect. A wrinkled hand holding another. A tree growing through concrete. Laughter during grief.

When we turn our attention toward beauty, we're not escaping reality—we're enhancing it. In a world that often trains us to spot flaws, cynicism, or failure, choosing to see beauty is a form of spiritual defiance.

It doesn't fix the world, but it changes how we walk through it.

What beauty might you be missing because you're focused on what's broken?

Tony D. Thelen

BRINGING IT TO LIFE

Beauty

- **Capture One Moment of Beauty Each Day.**

  Take a photo, write a note, or pause in silence to honor something beautiful you saw or felt today. Train your eyes to notice what uplifts.

- **Create a "Beauty Shelf" in Your Life.**

  Dedicate a small space—your desk, a shelf, or a corner—to objects, photos, or quotes that reflect beauty to you. Let it reset your gaze each day.

- **Speak Beauty into Someone's Life.**

  Offer an unexpected compliment that goes beyond appearance—point out something beautiful in someone's character, spirit, or effort.

- **Find Beauty in the Broken.**

  Choose one disappointment in your life and reflect: What has it taught you? Where has resilience, depth, or empathy emerged from it?

- **Schedule an Hour with No Purpose but Wonder.**

  Go on a walk, sit by water, or explore a museum—without a goal. Let beauty speak to you without needing to explain itself.

Beyond the Surface

A common misunderstanding about beauty is that it's purely physical or aesthetic—something superficial, skin-deep, or defined by trends and appearances.

In reality, beauty is a way of seeing—a deeper recognition of harmony, truth, and meaning in people, places, and moments. It's found in kindness, resilience, nature, connection, and even imperfection. True beauty stirs something within us—not because it conforms to a standard, but because it resonates with the soul. It's not about what you look at, but how you look.

WHAT'S ON MY MIND RIGHT NOW?

Beauty

Tony D. Thelen

Happiness

"Be cheerful. Strive to be happy."

In this simple yet profound directive, "Desiderata" acknowledges that happiness is not always spontaneous—it is often a practice. He doesn't say, "Be happy," as if it were effortless, but rather, "Strive to be."

This is a compassionate call to pursue joy not as a fleeting emotion, but as a steady, intentional posture. Cheerfulness becomes a courageous choice—a light we bring with us, not just something we wait to feel.

Happiness is not about denying sorrow, nor is it about shallow positivity. It's the quiet cultivation of gratitude, humor, resilience, and connection in the midst of life's complexity. In daily life, happiness reveals itself in small, honest joys: laughter with a friend, a deep breath of morning air, the feeling of purpose in doing something meaningful.

When we strive to be happy, we're not ignoring life's weight—we're balancing it. We are reminding ourselves that happiness is not found; it's made.

What would it look like to stop waiting for happiness and to begin actively creating it today?

> BRINGING IT TO LIFE

Happiness

- **Keep a Daily Joy Journal.**

    Each evening, write down three moments that brought you happiness, no matter how small. Train your brain to recognize and remember joy.

- **Schedule Something to Look Forward To.**

    Put one enjoyable, non-obligatory thing on your calendar each week. Anticipation is a powerful part of happiness.

- **Choose Cheerfulness in the Mundane.**

    Sing while doing dishes, smile at strangers, or play music while working. Bringing levity to ordinary tasks lifts your spirit and lightens your day.

- **Send a Happiness Ripple.**

    Text someone a sincere thank-you or compliment. Often, our own happiness deepens when we become the cause of someone else's.

- **Define Your "Happy Ingredients".**

    List the top five activities, people, or places that consistently boost your mood. Keep this list visible—and return to it regularly as part of your happiness practice.

Beyond the Surface

A common misunderstanding about happiness is that it's a constant state of pleasure, excitement, or ease—something you "achieve" when life is perfect, or problems disappear.

Happiness is often a byproduct of meaning, connection, and presence—not a destination, but a way of being. It's not about avoiding pain or chasing highs—it's about appreciating the moment, finding joy in simple things, and living in alignment with your values. True happiness can coexist with struggle, and it deepens through gratitude, purpose, and acceptance. It's less about what happens to you and more about how you engage with life.

WHAT'S ON MY MIND RIGHT NOW?

Happiness

Tony D. Thelen

THE RIVER CAREER & LIFE ASSESSMENT TM

As part of this book, you are entitled to take The River Career & Life Assessment™. This assessment was designed to model the themes that Ehrmann introduced in "Desiderata."

When you take the assessment, you will answer a series of questions on how well the statement applies to your life. The questions will take around ten to fifteen minutes to complete. Once you submit your responses, you will be given immediate feedback to the e-mail that you provided, including:

- High-level summary of your mindset, behavior, personal, and professional areas
- Overall scoring summary with your fulfillment index rankings
- Detailed feedback and recommendations with specific, actionable steps tailored to your responses

To access the assessment, scan the following URL code, and then use the password ""Desiderata"" when prompted.

https://tally.so/r/3lXeoN • Password = "desiderata"
(If the above link does not work, please e-mail tony@therivercoach.org)

THE MAN BEHIND THE POEM

Max Ehrmann was born on September 26, 1872, in Terre Haute, Indiana, the youngest of five children in a family of German descent. His parents had emigrated from Bavaria, and his father, a modest but intellectually curious man, ran a meat market. Though their means were limited, Ehrmann grew up in a household where literature and philosophy were valued. That early environment—blending the working-class ethic with a reverence for thought—would deeply shape Ehrmann's life and writing.

Ehrmann studied at DePauw University, a small liberal arts college in Indiana, where he distinguished himself as editor of the student newspaper and developed a lifelong fascination with philosophy, religion, and the human condition. After graduating in 1894, he pursued further studies at Harvard, where he was mentored by some of the most prominent thinkers of the day. Harvard's intellectual atmosphere left a deep impression on him, especially its blend of moral inquiry and rational thought, which would later influence his poetry.

Though Ehrmann harbored literary ambitions from a young age, he initially followed a more traditional career path. He returned to Terre Haute and practiced law for a time, then worked in the family business and later as a corporate counsel and vice president for a local manufacturing company. But even while immersed in legal briefs and commercial matters, Ehrmann wrote privately—essays, reflections, and poems that wrestled with questions of meaning, virtue, and peace.

By his forties, Ehrmann made a pivotal decision. He left his corporate job to devote himself entirely to writing. It was a bold move, especially for someone without the benefit of fame or financial security, but Ehrmann believed deeply in the power of words to inspire and heal. Over the following decades, he published numerous poems and prose works, most of them issued in small printings from his own press. Though he was never widely known in his lifetime, his writings found a quiet but loyal readership.

In 1927, Ehrmann wrote "Desiderata", which in Latin means "things to be desired." "Desiderata" was not published in a major outlet, nor did it create any immediate stir. Rather, it was quietly circulated among friends and admirers, many of whom were struck by its gentle, affirming tone. "Desiderata" was not a poem of grand literary ambition—it was a spiritual meditation, a piece of practical wisdom for navigating a noisy and often disorienting world.

Ehrmann died in 1945, never witnessing the worldwide embrace his words would eventually receive. In the decades following his death, "Desiderata" took on a life of its own. The poem was mistakenly attributed to an anonymous source and believed to have been discovered in Old St. Paul's Church in Baltimore, Maryland, in the seventeenth century. Nevertheless, the work resonated deeply with readers, especially during the turbulent 1960s and '70s. Its calm, grounded voice—offering counsel to "go placidly amid the noise and haste" and to "be gentle with yourself"—stood in stark contrast to the era's cultural chaos.

The poem was eventually copyrighted in Ehrmann's name by his widow, Bertha Ehrmann, and it began appearing in anthologies, greeting cards, posters, and classroom walls. It was recorded as a spoken-word single in 1971 by Les Crane and even charted on Billboard. Since then, "Desiderata" has become one of the most beloved modern meditations on life.

In the twenty-first century, "Desiderata" endures as a quiet cultural touchstone. It is quoted in graduation speeches, read at funerals, printed on bookmarks, and shared across digital platforms. Its appeal lies in its simplicity and timelessness. Without invoking specific ideologies or religious creeds, Ehrmann crafted a work that transcends divisions and speaks to a universal human longing—for peace, dignity, and purpose.

Today, Max Ehrmann is remembered not for the titles he held in business or law, but for the clarity and compassion of his words. In a world still marked by haste, conflict, and noise, his gentle exhortation to "be at peace with God, whatever you conceive Him to be" remains as relevant—and needed—as ever.

ABOUT THE AUTHOR

Tony Thelen is an executive coach, author, and founder of The River Coaching and Consulting, LLC. He focuses on removing pain, anxiety, and stress so leaders can focus on developing their ultimate potential in both professional and personal aspects of their lives. Drawing on more than thirty-five years of executive experience, Tony understands the challenges and opportunities that define modern leadership. His clients value his whole-life perspective, growth-oriented mindset, and steady advocacy.

Tony has coached leaders across six continents, guiding professionals at every stage of their careers in industries ranging from engineering and manufacturing to finance, strategy, technology, and start-ups. He is recognized for his ability to connect deeply with clients navigating high-stakes transitions, C-suite responsibilities, and the pursuit of success balanced with fulfillment.

He is also the author of Am I Doing This Right?: Foundations for a Successful Career and a Fulfilling Life, and he writes The River, a weekly professional development column syndicated in a growing number of newspapers. Tony holds a postgraduate diploma in Strategy and Innovation from the University of Oxford, an MBA from the University of Northern Iowa, and a bachelor's degree in Chemical Engineering from Iowa State University. In addition, he is certified in executive coaching by the NeuroLeadership Institute, accredited by the Co-Active Institute, trained in Hogan Assessments, affiliated with the International Coaching Federation, and a certified member of the CoachSource global executive coaching network.

About the Author

Tony lives in West Okoboji, Iowa, with his wife of more than thirty years. They are the proud parents of three grown daughters. When not coaching or writing, Tony enjoys fishing and engaging in conservation activities to preserve and protect the natural beauty of the Iowa Great Lakes.

Learn more at www.therivercoach.org or connect with Tony directly at tony@therivercoach.org.

www.ingramcontent.com/pod-product-compliance
Lightning Source LLC
Chambersburg PA
CBHW020546030426
42337CB00013B/983